Salon MASTERY

UNLOCKING THE PATH TO SUCCESS

Salon MASTERY

UNLOCKING THE PATH TO SUCCESS

Ankit Virmani
Subham Virmani

Worldwide Published by
Pendown Press

PENDOWN PRESS LLP
An ISO 9001 & ISO 14001 Certified Co.,
Regd. Office: 3767A, Kanhaiya Nagar,
Tri Nagar, Delhi-110035
Ph.: 8130886000, 9650072927
E-mail: info@pendownpress.com
Branch Office: 1A/2A, 20, Hari Sadan, Ansari Road,
Daryaganj, New Delhi-110002
Ph.: 011-45794768
Website: PendownPress.com

Edition: 2024
Price: ₹ 399
ISBN: 978-93-6338-041-7

Layout and Cover Designed by Pendown Graphics Team
Printed and Bound in India by Thomson Press India Ltd.

CONTENTS

Acknowledgements

First and foremost, we would like to thank our **parents**, who gave us abundant love and provided a nurturing environment during our early childhood years, which enabled us to grow up as independent and self-confident entrepreneurs.

Secondly, we would like to thank our respective **spouses,** who have enabled us to spend weeks and days on our travels for our business meetings, while taking care of the family and our children.

To our amazing **team**—past and present—thank you for being our partners in this journey. Your dedication, creativity, and passion have helped us reach out to the market and make a positive change in the growth of the salons. You've taught us as much as we have taught you, and together, together we've built something truly special.

A special thank you to our **mentors and colleagues** in the industry. Your wisdom, guidance, and willingness to share your experiences have been invaluable and we are forever grateful.

To our **clients**, thank you for trusting us & allowing me to be part of your journey. Your loyalty and feedback have inspired us to continually evolve, innovate, and strive for excellence. You are the reason this industry is so meaningful.

Lastly, to the **readers** of this book—whether you are a salon owner, stylist, or someone aspiring to be part of the beauty industry—thank you for taking the time to invest in your future. We are confident that the insights and lessons in these pages will help you unlock your own path to success.

Meet Your Authors
Ankit & Subham Virmani
The Salon Growth Experts

ANKIT VIRMANI is the ***visionary Director of Esskay Beauty Resources,*** a leading name in India's professional hair and beauty industry since 2002. Armed with a postgraduate degree in finance and international business, Ankit has travelled extensively, visiting over 20 countries and 100 cities to gain unparalleled insights into the global salon trade.

Ankit's groundbreaking introduction of Rica Lipo Waxes from Italy revolutionised the Indian waxing experience, setting new standards for consumer comfort and satisfaction. His expertise is backed by a wealth of knowledge from various global courses in marketing, business strategy, and development, making him India's leading Salon Growth Expert.

A prolific author, Ankit regularly contributes to industry publications through blogs and articles, sharing his deep knowledge with a wider audience. His insights have also made him a sought-after speaker at both government and international forums. An avid traveller and technology enthusiast, Ankit's blend of industry experience and forward-thinking vision continues to shape the beauty landscape of India.

SUBHAM VIRMANI, ***Director of Sales & Strategy at Esskay Beauty Resources***, has been a driving force in India's salon industry for over 15 years. With a Post Graduate degree in Family Managed Business from SP Jain Institute of Management & Research, Mumbai, Subham has travelled to more than 15 countries, immersing himself in global salon trends and gaining insights from renowned educators.

A true leader in the field, Subham has conducted educational seminars and workshops in over 50 cities across India, empowering more than 3,000 students with strategies for salon business growth and brand partnerships. His expertise has made him a sought-after speaker at esteemed trade conferences such as Professional Beauty, Images Group, Cosmoprof, and Beauty Launchpad.

As a thought leader, Subham has penned numerous articles on salon growth strategy, and featured in leading trade publications like Salon International, Style Speak, Femina Salon & Spa, and Beauty Launchpad. His passion for giving back is evident in his role as an advisory board member of the non-profit organisation Beautiful Hearts Fund, which supports families in the wellness industry during times of crisis.

Subham is also pioneering a 'Green Revolution in Salons,' focusing on sustainable practices and promoting eco-friendly products. Outside work, he is a passionate traveller, avid networker, and dedicated music producer. A strong believer in Sahaja Yoga meditation since 1998, Subham's mantra for success is simple yet powerful: "Always be grateful and face every situation in life with a smile." His unwavering positivity and holistic approach to life and business continue to inspire those around him.

Preface

The beauty industry is more than just styling hair or enhancing appearances—it's about crafting experiences, building relationships, and creating a lasting impact on both clients and the team.

Being in this industry for over 22 years, we have seen firsthand how the right blend of artistry, business acumen, and personal growth can unlock the true potential of a salon business. It's not just about working hard but working smart, and that's what *Salon Mastery* is all about.

This book was born out of our passion as Growth Partners to Salons across the country. Along this journey, we faced many challenges, learned hard lessons, and discovered strategies that we learnt while observing salons and interacting with salon owners on how to survive and thrive in this competitive industry.

We are excited to share these insights with you because we understand that with the right guidance, every salon owner or stylist has the power to unlock success.

In *Salon Mastery*, **we explore the critical elements that take a salon from average to extraordinary**—whether it's mastering customer service, improving staff retention, increasing revenue, or creating a brand that stands out in a crowded marketplace.

Our goal is to provide you with proven strategies that you can implement right away and start seeing the changes in your results

Whether you're just starting out, looking to expand your salon, or hoping to refine and perfect your business operations, this book will provide you with a roadmap to success.

It's not just about making more money—though that's important—but about building a sustainable, fulfilling, and profitable career that you're proud of.

Thank you for picking up this book. We are sure it will inspire and empower you to master your salon business and unlock a path to lasting success.

Sincerely,

Ankit & Subham Virmani
Directors, Esskay Beauty

Why This Book?

Putting Things Into Perspective

Most salons in India began as startups from a journey that evolved into becoming business owners from being hairdressers, make-up artists or beauty professionals.

What started as an informal and casual business, over the years has seen tremendous growth, fame and profitability. However, due to humble beginnings, most salons have learnt to manage their business from wisdom learnt through years of experience.

As the Directors of Esskay Beauty, a company dedicated to providing high-quality products to salons, we've had the privilege of working closely with **thousands of salon owners, stylists, and beauty professionals from all walks of life in over 100 cities, across 20 countries & have gained an understanding of strategies that most successful salons have in common.**

Over the years, we've observed a recurring challenge: many salons, despite their passion and talent, struggle to achieve sustainable success. Whether it's navigating the complexities of managing a business, retaining clients, or staying ahead of industry trends, the path to mastering a salon business can be daunting. Salon Mastery – Unlock Path to Success was written to address these very challenges. This book is not just a guide to improving your salon's profitability; it's a comprehensive roadmap to creating a business that thrives on innovation, customer loyalty, and long-term growth. We have worked to create a resource that speaks directly to those looking to elevate their business.

The intention of sharing the success strategies in this book stems from the love, respect and fame that this industry has blessed us and our company with. We believe that by sharing this knowledge we will empower salon entrepreneurs to manage and grow their businesses more effectively.

The core philosophy and focus of our company has always been education as a means of empowerment. We have been imparting education in the hair and beauty industry since 2002 to thousands of hairdressers and beauticians. This book is merely a continuation of that philosophy to give back to the community that has given us so much.

We believe that success in the beauty industry goes beyond offering great services. It requires a deep understanding of business strategies, effective use of products, and creating an environment where both clients and staff feel valued. This book is designed to provide salon owners and professionals with actionable insights, proven strategies, and the mindset needed to unlock their full potential.

If you're passionate about your salon and ready to take it to the next level, this book will serve as your guide. It will empower you to overcome obstacles, seize opportunities, and build a salon that stands out in a crowded market.

So get ready to learn and implement the proven strategies that super-successful salon entrepreneurs implement.

Here's to scaling up your business and successful salon mastery!

Together, let's unlock the path to lasting success.

Chapter 1

The Salon Industry Landscape in 2024

Nothing conveys the big picture of an industry as figures do, so let's begin the journey to salon mastery by taking a look at some facts & figures —

The Indian Beauty Salon Market: The Big Picture

- **The Indian Beauty Salon Market** was valued at **USD 11.65 Billion (approx. ₹99,000 Crores)** in **2024**
- It is expected to reach **USD 22.99 Billion (approx. ₹1,95,000 Crores)** by **2033**, at a **CAGR of 7.85%** during the forecast period **2024 – 2033.**

Now that we have taken a look at the potential of this industry, the next logical step is to define briefly what a beauty salon broadly means.

Defining A Beauty Salon

A beauty salon is a facility where individuals can receive various cosmetic treatments and services aimed at enhancing their physical appearance, typically including hair care, skin care, nail care, and other aesthetic procedures.

**Source: Custom Market Insights*

Some Fun Facts/Data: The Number of Salons & Spending

- No. of Organised Salons (Estimated): 1,50,000+
- [There is still a very big unorganised segment]
- India's Average Salon Spending: US$6 (Approx ₹ 505)
- Global Average Salon Spend: US$35 (Approx ₹ 3000)

Seeing the above data, it is clear that the average spending in India is quite low compared to global averages.

There is still a huge opportunity to grow the business with various factors that include –

- A growing middle class with higher disposable incomes.
- A young population with growing aspirations.
- Growing consumerism and influence from the Western world.
- Easier credit availability with access to organised credit with credit cards, and EMIs, as the economy is digitalising and is being organised.
- A growing fashion and grooming sense with increased exposure to social media channels.

Also, it is evident from the above data that the industry will double over the next 10 years, it's the right moment and time to be invested in the salon business and also continue to innovate and grow to take advantage of the immense growth potential that the industry offers.

Access to & availability of a trained and skilled workforce is the biggest concern that salons are facing. With limited staff and not many avenues for good training, salon owners are struggling to maintain the quality of their services.

Most of the staff evolves and improves based on first-hand learning by working in the salon. A big portion and responsibility of training the workforce lies with the brands that work in the professional space and provide brand education and skill development classes.

The business of academies of hairdressing and beauty is doing well and many players are organising themselves and growing their presence across regions and nationally as well. Some of these academies are run by corporates and others are led by experienced artists who may be also running their own salons and offering training academy services.

The demand outlook in the salon industry is strong.

There is great protentional in Tier 2 and Tier 3 and other interior cities across the country where in some cases, salons are still being run in home setups in traditional styles. The demand for good products is building and growing in the interiors of the country.

Key segments driving this growth include **hair care services**, which remain culturally important and consistently in demand due to evolving fashion trends and the influence of social media. **Skincare services**, such as facials and anti-ageing treatments, are also gaining prominence, reflecting increased consumer awareness of skin health and beauty routines. Additionally, **nail care services** are experiencing rapid adoption, particularly among younger urban consumers, fuelled by trends on social media.

Salon chains are capitalizing on these trends by expanding into smaller cities and offering diverse services, which are expected to attract a broader customer base.

❍ ❍ ❍ ❍

Chapter 2

The Changing Landscape — Early Days to Modern Salons

Nowadays it's not women alone who contribute to the salon business. The men's customer base is a very fast-growing segment that is willing to undergo more advanced services than just a haircut and colour as in the past.

The landscape of salons in India has undergone significant changes over the years, driven by evolving consumer preferences, economic growth, and shifts in lifestyle.

Here are some key insights on how the salon industry has changed over the years -

The Journey From Traditional Beauty Parlors and Barber Shops to Modern Salons

In the early years, the basic salon and grooming services in India were offered by local barbers and beauticians, often in small, basic setups usually from their homes. There was one small room dedicated to these services and often people from the nearby locality used to visit the salon for basic services. Unisex beauty salons were a rarity (in fact, they didn't exist, to begin with), mostly they were *Ladies Beauty Parlours* and *Men's Barber Hair Cutting Salons.* Millennials and older age groups would recall such salon setups.

During that period some products such as hair removal waxes, were usually made at home and used. International brands were hardly present in any segment.

I recall that people often used to travel to larger metro cities such as Delhi or Mumbai to visit the more modern salons and preferred to go there for more advanced services, as per their desires.

Nowadays, in the last two decades, there has been a huge shift towards modern salons that offer 360-degree services including haircare, hair cuts, skincare, nail care, spa treatments, makeup and many more.

These are now modern unisex setups (mostly), that offer comfort, plush interiors and branded products with well-trained and educated staff. **It is a completely different experience from that offered in the past.** Some of the organized chains are offering luxurious spaces, with a high level of hospitality and offer a great experience with choices of branded products and services.

These salons have now become more holistic destinations for consumers and people prefer to go there not just for the specific services but for the holistic experience, to unwind and relax.

A very important part of the credit for organizing the industry goes to the product brands that have provided the salons with global exposure and helped them in marketing their services to the customers. These brands have also provided education and training to the workforce in this segment such as ***hairdressers and beauty professionals*** to upskill them and also helped the salons get organised and offer better experiences to their clients.

The Indian salon industry has evolved from a largely unorganized sector to a thriving, dynamic industry characterized by innovation, specialization, and a focus on customer experience. This transformation reflects broader changes in Indian society, including rising aspirations, changing lifestyles, and increased awareness of personal grooming and wellness.

India is one of the few countries in the world that has such diverse salon setups that offer hair, beauty, nail and makeup services all under one roof. In the USA and Europe, these kind of services are offered by at least 3 different business . **Modern salons in India offer a holistic destination for all services under one roof.**

The salon industry in India is diverse, offering a range of services tailored to different beauty and wellness needs.

The primary types of salons in India are -

1. ***Exclusive Hair Salons:*** These are the most common type of salons in India, offering services like haircuts, hair styling, colouring, and various hair treatments such as keratin or scalp therapies. Hair salons cater to both men and women and are heavily influenced by fashion trends and social media. They are often artist-driven and usually the salon owner is the hair artist themself.
2. ***Beauty Salons:*** These salons specialize in skincare treatments, including facials, waxing, anti-ageing therapies, acne treatments, skin rejuvenation and also a variety of body treatments. They have seen a rise in demand due to increasing consumer awareness of skin health and wellness. In some countries, they are also referred to as Aesthetic Centres.
3. ***Nail Salons:*** Nail care is a fast-growing segment in India, offering services like manicures, pedicures, nail art, and nail extensions. Nail salons are popular among younger consumers and are driven by fashion trends and social media.
4. ***Spa Salons:*** These establishments focus on relaxation and rejuvenation through services like massages, body treatments, and wellness therapies. Spa salons often blend traditional Indian wellness practices with modern spa techniques. Some of them

offer more advanced body services as well such as slimming and other advanced body therapies.

5. ***Full-Service Salons:*** These salons offer a wide range of services, including hair, skin, and nail care, along with makeup and grooming services. They cater to both men and women, providing a one-stop shop for all beauty needs. This is the most common type of salon in India.

6. ***Men's Grooming Salons:*** These cater specifically to men's grooming needs, offering haircuts, beard styling, and specialized skincare treatments. The demand for men's grooming services has grown significantly in recent years.

7. ***At-Home Salons:*** At-home salons in India have gained significant popularity in recent years, especially due to the demand for convenience and personalized services. These are tech-driven platforms which are targeting the convenience of consumers.

All the segments have their unique potential as well as challenges. It is best advised to survey the area and meet some consumers to better understand which model will be the right model for the salon to adopt in each region. The salon models may vary depending on the area.

❍ ❍ ❍ ❍

Chapter 3

Client Acquisition and Retention: The Doorway To Success

Once you have decided on the business model or are already operating a salon, this is one of the most important parts of the book for you.

Acquiring and retaining clients is critical for the success of any salon business.

I am breaking this into 2 parts for easier understanding and implementation–

We will delve into Client Acquisition and Client Retention in detail individually.

A. *Client Acquisition* –

The first step in any client acquisition strategy is working on where your traffic will come from.

- Do you already own a database that you can work on to acquire new customers?
- Or you need to acquire the data right from scratch from external sources.

If you are already running a salon then it's best to use your gold mine, your own database, and start to communicate with them. You can look at ways to reactivate the old/lost clients and activate them.

The most crucial thing here is what and how you communicate with them. It is extremely crucial to research your market and understand the needs and desires of your customers. It is often achieved by interviewing some consumers of your area or customers of your competitors, on why they are patronising a particular salon. You will be surprised to know that if you read between the lines, they will spill the secret of their why of visiting a particular salon and it will help you to understand the market needs and desires and create your marketing message that helps bring the customer to your world – **YOUR SALON.**

Some of the most effective client acquisition strategies include -

1. ***Referral Programs***

    - ***Word-of-Mouth Marketing:*** Encourage existing clients to refer friends and family by offering discounts or free services for successful referrals. Word-of-mouth remains one of the most powerful tools for acquiring new clients and is often the most under utilised.

2. ***Online Presence and Digital Marketing***

    - ***Social Media:*** Utilize platforms like Instagram, and Facebook, to showcase your work, promote special offers, and engage with potential clients. High-quality images and videos of your services can attract attention and drive bookings. Videos and Reels offer great content that engages with the audience and helps get their attention to your salon.

    - ***Google My Business:*** Ensure your salon is listed on Google My Business with accurate information, photos, and client reviews. This improves local search visibility and makes it easier for new clients to find you. Always keep the profile updated with correct contact numbers, and opening and closing times and don't forget to mention the holidays on the calendar.

***NOTE:** Please keep a regular tab on your reviews and posts that your clients are posting. It will help you understand the quality of services you are offering. Any negative review should be taken with a learner's mindset that will help you improve and work upon the mistakes that caused them. It's important to take insights from them and improve your business process and delivery.

3. ***Partnerships and Collaborations***
    - ***Collaborate with other related businesses:*** Collaborate with nearby businesses such as gyms, spas, or fashion boutiques to offer joint promotions to their customers. For example, a discount at your salon for clients of a partnering boutique. It will help you get traffic from consumers from other businesses and give them a chance to experience your services.
    - ***Events and Pop-Ups:*** Participate in local events or set up pop-up booths at shopping centres, malls, and melas. festivals, or community events to introduce your salon to a new audience.
4. ***Introductory Offers***
    - ***Discounts or Special Deals for New Clients:*** Offer special discounts or packages for first-time clients to encourage them to try your services.
    - ***Service Bundles:*** Create attractive service bundles that offer value, such as a haircut and facial at a discounted rate, to draw in new clients. This a great way to upsell and cross-sell your services and increase the average order value of your salon.
5. ***Online Booking and Convenience***
    - ***User-Friendly Booking:*** Make it easy for clients to book appointments online via your website or app. Offering convenience can attract tech-savvy clients who prefer digital solutions. This is a growing trend in most countries. Of course, on-call booking is equally encouraged and should be offered.
    - ***App for Booking and E-Commerce:*** Some salons have launched their own apps that encourage you to book appointments

from it for a more seamless experience. These apps also have a members zone, where you can buy retail products and services at either a member's discounted rate or accumulate reward points that later get converted to money or free services.

6. ***Targeted Advertising***

    - ***Social Media and Google Ads:*** Run targeted ads on social media platforms to reach specific demographics based on age, location, interests, and more. Invest in local SEO and Google Ads to capture clients searching for salons in your area.

It is prudent to invest in a good digital marketing agency that can assist you with creatives and also advise you on best advertising and marketing strategies and provide you with leads to acquire new customers. Take into account the Budget and cost of each lead that you are paying. Also, give regular feedback to them on the quality of the leads that you are getting. Keep a trained tele-calling – client relations team to work and convert those leads and help you in acquiring new clients.

B. Client Retention -

Fun Fact

52.5% of the respondents are having a relationship span with their salon for 1-3 Years –

Customer Loyalty is the Key!

Let's understand that it is the customer that is paying our bills. Some people look at customers with a very short-term mindset. The moment a client walks in the door, we all start seeing how much we can sell to him/her.

The first part that I would like to explain here is that we have to change this mindset and start focusing on being **useful and of value to them.**

Before jumping to business discussions, make them seated and comfortable and let them get accustomed to the salon environment. A cosy seating will be very helpful in making them feel welcomed and also offer them a beverage of their choice.

One example of being useful can be offering them genuine advice on what services work best for them irrespective of their price point.

The moment we start doing that we will start building a meaningful trustful relationship with them and it will be our first step towards client retention.

This is a very deep understanding that should be instilled not only in the owner but all the staff working in the salon or whoever the customers interact with.

The next step is taking them through the menu card and understanding their requirements and expectations. Once the client has expressed their requirement, we should start the consultation on the most suitable services or products that best cater to their needs.

Since the menu has a variety of services of the same category at multiple price points, we should offer the best to them. It is important to ask the right questions and also understand about any allergies or sensitivity to any ingredient or brand product.

Another important thing to be kept in mind should be asking for their feedback on the services provided. Were they satisfied? Did it live up to their expectation?

Observe and act on any feedback that the client expresses to understand what improvements can be made in the service delivery based on the feedback.

Fun Fact

Approximately 92.5% of the Clients recommend the salon to their friends and family if they are happy with the services and the products –

One happy client can recommend and bring another 4-5 clients on referrals.

Make each client's experience AWESOME!

Let me explain this with an example:

The Chaos Resulting From A Wrong Consultation & Offering

Imagine a client named Ishika, a selective client who is extremely particular about what brands she uses and what ingredients her skin is accustomed to, walked into a salon and asked for a facial service. Imagine if the staff did not consult her on her skin type and sensitivity, and instead jumped to offering her a facial of a particular brand starting from the most expensive facial on the menu, just because they have its stock and have a good deal with the company or simply more profit. Imagine the outcome if her skin got irritated and she felt uncomfortable, the chaos that would be created in the salon and also the reviews and negative referrals that the salon would get. Hence it's extremely important to have the right consultation built into the service offering.

Now that we have context on the importance of customer retention, let us deep dive into a few strategies -

1. ***Loyalty Programs***
   - ***Reward Points:*** Implement a loyalty program where clients earn points for each visit or service. Points can be redeemed for discounts, free services, or products. In order to introduce

this and have a good response, please sell the membership either for free on a certain value of services or a very lucrative low price point that allows them to get discounts or points on the very first billing. The best way to sell is during the time when the customer is making payment for the services availed on that day.

- ***Tiered Rewards:*** Offer tiered loyalty levels, where clients who visit more frequently or spend more receive higher-tier rewards such as exclusive discounts or priority bookings.
- ***Some salons are also selling Membership packages*** for Rs. 20,000/- to about Rs. 1,00,000/- where they get unlimited services on high ticket value or about 30% - 50% more value credit on the services that can be availed in a certain period of time.

2. ***Personalized Experience***

- ***Client Records:*** Keep detailed records of each client's preferences, past services, and product purchases. Use this information to offer personalized recommendations and ensure consistency in service. This goes a long way in making the client feel special.
- ***Birthday and Anniversary Offers:*** Send personalized messages with special discounts or complimentary services on clients' birthdays or anniversaries to make them feel valued. This forms a very important part of your Keep In Touch Strategy. Keep in mind to communicate as per the medium of their choice – Call, SMS, WhatsApp, Email, etc.

3. ***Consistent Quality of Service***

- ***Staff Training:*** Regularly train your staff to maintain high service standards. Happy clients who consistently receive excellent service are more likely to return.
- ***Product Quality:*** Use high-quality products and tools to

ensure the best results for your clients, as this builds trust and satisfaction. This is an extremely crucial point and this makes or breaks the client's experience. Always make sure you are using Professional Products only, that are not readily available in the retail market. Go for a standard brand, that offers good quality products as per the price bracket of the services that you are offering.

- Always plan your inventory and be well stocked on Professional as well as Retail products. You don't want to run out of stock for an important product when the customer is sitting on the chair and demanding the service.

4. ***Client Feedback and Engagement***

- ***Surveys and Reviews:*** Ask for feedback after each visit and encourage clients to leave reviews online. Responding to reviews, both positive and negative, shows that you care about your clients' opinions. Always have the QR codes displayed at the reception counter to get reviews.
- ***Regular Communication:*** Stay in touch with clients through newsletters, SMS, or WhatsApp messages about upcoming offers, new services, or salon news. There can be multiple occasions you can be in touch with them.

Some of the messaging occasions can be –

- Festival Wishes
- New Brand or Service Launches
- Reward Points and Transaction Messages
- Invitation to Events
- Reminder Calls and Messages to visit the salon based on their previous visit frequency.
- New and engaging Social Media content... and many more

5. ***Membership Plans***

- ***Subscription Models:*** Offer monthly or yearly membership plans that provide regular services at a discounted rate. This not only ensures repeat visits but also provides a steady stream of revenue. Some salons are offering membership plans that can be used by the entire family. So it helps in getting the business of the entire family instead of just one individual.

6. ***Exclusive Offers and VIP Events***

- ***VIP Events:*** Host exclusive events for loyal clients, such as product launches, workshops, or special sales. Giving them early access to new services or products makes them feel special and valued. Please plan these events with your brand partners and they will be willing to participate in this activity.
- ***Limited-Time Offers:*** Run exclusive deals for repeat clients that are not available to the general public. Many salons offer rate cards with 2 kinds of pricing – Non Member and Member (Discounted) Rates that encourage the clients to take the membership plan.

7. ***Environment and Ambiance***

- ***Comfortable and Inviting Atmosphere:*** Create a salon environment that is comfortable, relaxing, and aesthetically pleasing. Clients are more likely to return to a place where they feel pampered and relaxed.
- ***Refreshments and Amenities:*** Offer complimentary refreshments, Wi-Fi, or other amenities that enhance the client experience.

8. ***Follow-Up and Aftercare***

- ***Post-Service Follow-Up:*** Send a thank-you message after each visit, along with tips for maintaining their new look. This can help build a stronger relationship with the client.

- ***Aftercare Packages:*** Offer aftercare products or kits that clients can purchase to maintain the results of their salon services.

By combining these client acquisition and retention strategies, salons can build a strong, loyal customer base while continually attracting new clients, leading to sustained growth and success.

Fun Fact

Statistics show that over 55% of inactive clients can become active if they are contacted again!

It costs more time and money to generate a new client than to bring back an old one.

Do you know your Client Attrition Rate?

- Attrition Rate refers to the percentage of clients you lose or those who become inactive.
- Most Salon Owners write off inactive clients as lost clients and do not even track their attrition rate.

Getting back your lost clients!

Focus on the 3 R's –

The 3 R's is a proven technique that works on the science of winning back your inactive clients. Let us look at this framework below -

1. ***Referral:*** Remember 92.5% of Clients recommend to their family and friends.

   Make use of Gift Vouchers, Referral Cards and Discount Vouchers

2. ***Retention:*** remember 83% of clients are visiting the Salon and Spa on a monthly basis.

   Track the Lifetime Client Value, Membership and Bundled Packages

3. ***Reactivation:*** Have you reached out to your clients who have not come back?

   Track your lost customers, offer them some Free Service and call them every 8 weeks of inactivity.

Let's understand the 3R framework, with some examples,

- ***Referrals :*** The best way to use a referral can be to reward the client with a discount card or a free service or product (that adds value to them) for every referred client who has visited the salon. This can be a big motivation factor for the client and she would then make it a point to recommend it to her entire social circle.
- ***Retention :*** The best example can be to offer them packages for each service. Example – Based on skin consultation, offer them a facial treatment package for every 2 weeks. You can bundle them into a discount package. Book 3 facials and get 1 free or pay for 3 facials and get some retail product free for maintaining the result at home. These packages would definitely tie the client with your salon and also a regular visitor. Once the client visits for a facial service, you can upsell or cross-sell other services that the client wants, like Waxing or pedicure, etc for increased invoice value.
- Another example of Retention can be Client Membership. The membership should be introduced at a very low price point and a certain value should be immediately redeemable at the time of paying the bill. If you notice this is happening all around us. All the food delivery apps, E-Commerce apps, all are offering memberships at nominal rates with immediate benefits. It helps in not making the client think too much and immediately go for the membership. Some salons also allow the membership to be shared

amongst family members to bring their business to the salon as well. So by selling 1 membership, you are getting 3 to 4 clients' loyalty to the salon.

- ***Reactivation :*** Have you organised your clients in a database based on their frequency of visits? Or the services they require regularly? It is a good practice to keep an organised database using the CRM software and send information about new launches and also some interesting content that keeps reminding them about your existence. The market is dynamic, salon business works on proximity.
- Sending service reminders or reminders with discounts if the visit is delayed is a good practice that often reaps great results.

Give some thought to it and understand and evaluate your Keep In Touch Strategy **(KIT) strategy and your relationship with your client.**

Some Key Points for the KIT Strategy can be summarised as below –

- Focus on building strong relationships first
- Target the right people
- Target the right people at the right time
- Target the right people at the right time with the right message
- Target the right people at the right time with the right message promoting the right product.
- Analyse the results and make the necessary changes.
- Repeat the cycle

Do make it a point to evaluate and Implement your Keep In Touch Strategy!!

Chapter 4

The Salon Menu: A Powerful Business Tool

Focus on the Salon Menu as a **Sales tool.**

- Each Service Item should be descriptive, so the right expectations are set before the service starts for maximum customer satisfaction.
- Trust me, this is the first tangible collateral that all the clients go through. Make it as luxurious as you would like to hold it.
- Simplicity and clarity of design are important. Remember to maintain the visual hierarchy, the order in which the human eye perceives what it sees.

Don't Forget The Hick's Law

Also, another very important aspect to keep in mind is – The Hick's Law.

Hick's Law states that the client is initially attracted to a broad variety of choices, but if the choices exceed a certain threshold, they freeze up and are confused to arrive at a purchase decision. So keep the choices relevant but to a minimum and focus on building the business on those choices.

- A strong **About Us Page** establishing the **Authority of the Salon** and its Key Members is essential. Always highlight the key members of your team such as the Creative Director or Art Director. By building on those, you build authority in your area, and it adds to the trust level in the minds of your consumers.

- ***Expert Tip: Showcase your original creative work with Posters in the Salons and the menu.***
- Maintain a presentation of **Before and After Pics** of Facial Treatments and Hair Services to build clients' trust and also a benchmark for matching their expectations. Please note, do not exaggerate the Before / After pics and provide a disclaimer that the results may vary from client to client. You can also prepare a special book showing these results.
- Offer a good balance of **Basic, Premium and Luxury Services** with rates displayed for members and non-members for all categories.
- By offering services at multiple price points, you can cater to a wide variety of clients at multiple price points, based on their spending capacity. Also usually the premium and luxury brands have products with better and higher actives so they can get you great results. Entry Category brands are great for entry-level, low-duration services. Often the clients do not have enough time and is in a rush, for such a client a Basic Service often work the best.

Pro Tip

One mistake to avoid here is to offer the same brands for different segments. **Eg. Premium and Luxury categories should not have the same brand or at least the same product line.** Otherwise the client feels that he/she is getting the same \ service at higher rates. It is only through brand differentiation that this concept works.

- Introduce lucrative Add On Cross-Selling services to Basic Services to increase profitability!

Go Green Or Go Out!

Introduce a **Special Section for Sustainable, Green and Organic Services** as it is the fastest-growing category globally.

As per KPMG, the Organic and Green beauty market is likely to reach US$ 1.7 billion by 2025. Globally it is the biggest growth driver for the salon industry.

The Economist had appointed 2019 as the year of the Vegan. Vegan and organic has now turned mainstream.

Particularly, more and more consumers are opting for alcohol-free, delicate skin products, hypoallergenic or allergen-free, not tested on animals.

Veganism is a thriving lifestyle, and a growing number of people are embracing it, to the point that it is spreading into several lifestyles. The growing ethical consumption is therefore giving a boost to the demand for vegan cosmetics.

There is a range of Natural and Organic products and services available in the market. The range starts from Facials and waxing and ranges to Hair Care, Treatments and Colours. Having specific services based around the Organic and Natural categories is a must-have for any offering.

Do look at your Salon Menu and evaluate it ....!!

Does it provide all the information you would like to receive?

If not, take action to modify, update and upgrade it, otherwise, you are missing out on leveraging one of your most powerful business tools.

❍ ❍ ❍ ❍

Chapter 5

Standing Head & Shoulders Above The Competition Locally

Fun Fact

58.8% of the respondents are coming back to the salon because it is near to their residence.

- Location is the most important aspect!

Ensure Strong Marketing for Brand Building in your area.

The Neighbourhood is one of the most important decisions you will make for your salon. It has a huge influence on your business. There is a strong reason that you should work on building the authority of your salon in your area.

You should plan marketing activities and reach out within your target market area. Doing regular celebration or promotion days in your salon also increases the outreach in your area.

Since there are many competition salons in a popular neighbourhood, it is important that you identify the right consumer for targeted reach.

Whether your client is in the Premium Category or Luxury category or is your core specialisation Hair, Skin or Makeup focused. Having a clear focus and communication will work best among your clients. Remember, you cannot specialise in all segments of your salon. It will be too general. If you focus on Hair or Skin, it does not mean you do not offer other services. There is a spillover effect over the services and the client prefers to get all services under one roof. With this specialisation, you can shield your salon against your competition in the neighbourhood.

Here are strategies that salons can use to stay ahead of the competition:

1. ***Focus on Unique Selling Proposition (USP)***
   - ***Identify and Highlight Your USP:*** Determine what sets your salon apart from others in the area. This could be a unique service, specialized treatments, premium products, or an exceptional customer experience. Make sure your USP is clearly communicated in all your marketing materials.
   - ***Examples:*** Offering organic or cruelty-free products, exclusive services like bridal makeup, or a highly personalized customer experience.
2. ***Maintain High Service Quality***
   - ***Consistent Service Standards:*** Ensure that every client receives top-notch service, regardless of which stylist or beautician they work with. Regular staff training is essential to maintain consistent quality.
   - ***Attention to Detail:*** Small touches, like remembering clients' preferences or offering a complimentary beverage or a top-up service, can make a big difference in customer satisfaction.
3. ***Build Strong Relationships with Clients***
   - ***Personalized Communication:*** Use client data to send personalized offers, birthday discounts, or appointment reminders. Building a personal connection with your clients fosters loyalty.
   - ***Loyalty Programs:*** Implement a loyalty program that rewards repeat visits, referrals, and high spending. This encourages

clients to return to your salon instead of trying a competitor.

4. ***Invest in Staff Training and Development***
   - ***Skill Enhancement:*** Regularly train your staff on the latest trends, techniques, and products. Skilled professionals attract clients and can differentiate your salon from others.
   - ***Employee Satisfaction:*** Happy and motivated employees provide better service. Offer competitive compensation, growth opportunities, and a positive work environment.
5. ***Competitive Pricing Strategy***
   - ***Value Over Price:*** Competing solely on price can be risky. Instead, focus on offering value. Ensure that clients perceive they are getting excellent service and results for the price they pay. Another aspect to look forward to is not getting into the discount trap. There may be cases in the neighbourhood salon is offering a 50% discount all year round or 1+1 services. Please understand that it's a trap. Such salons might offer services with low-quality products, or they may misguide their clients on their product usage. This is a short-term tactic and usually does not last long. It is OK to have time-based promotions to keep your client engaged. But year-round activity will lower the positioning of your salon, and it will be hard to come out from it.
   - ***Tiered Pricing:*** Offer a range of services at different price points to cater to various client segments. For example, premium services for those willing to pay more and basic services for budget-conscious clients.
6. ***Leverage Digital Marketing***
   - ***Social Media Engagement:*** Actively engage with your audience on social media platforms like Instagram, Facebook, and Pinterest. Showcase your work, share client testimonials, and promote special offers. Influencer-based marketing can

be another idea that works wonders in your area. If you have an influencer or a client that has a good social following, you can utilise their network and use it spread awareness about your salon. Offering them a free service and asking them to post about it on social media is a great way to gain popularity in your region.

- ***Content Marketing:*** Create valuable content, such as blogs or video tutorials on hair care, skincare, or beauty trends. This positions your salon as an expert in the industry and attracts new clients.

7. ***Offer Exceptional Customer Experience***

    - ***Ambiance and Comfort:*** Create a welcoming and relaxing salon environment. The overall experience, from the moment clients walk in, should be enjoyable and memorable.
    - ***Efficient Operations:*** Minimize wait times and ensure smooth appointment scheduling. An efficient experience keeps clients happy and reduces frustration.

8. ***Monitor Competitors***

    - ***Stay Informed:*** Regularly check what your competitors are offering in terms of services, pricing, and promotions. This allows you to adjust your strategies proactively.
    - ***Learn and Innovate:*** Take inspiration from your competitors' successes and learn from their mistakes. Innovate your offerings based on market trends and client needs.

9. ***Diversify Your Services***

    - ***Add-On Services:*** Offer complementary services that add value, such as head massages with haircuts or skincare consultations with facials. This not only increases revenue per client but also differentiates your salon.
    - ***Seasonal and Trend-Based Services:*** Introduce limited-time

services based on seasonal needs or beauty trends. This keeps your offerings fresh and exciting.

10. ***Collect and Act on Feedback***

- ***Customer Feedback:*** Regularly seek feedback from clients to understand their needs and preferences. Act on this feedback to improve your services and address any shortcomings.
- ***Online Reviews:*** Encourage satisfied clients to leave positive reviews on platforms like Google or Facebook. Positive reviews can significantly influence potential clients in choosing your salon over competitors.

11. ***Customer Testimonials*** - Testimonials are another great example that works very well. Taking testimonials of happy clients and playing them on a TV screen or your social media page, also allows the prospects to win the trust that the services offered are world-class and they can trust the salon for their services. Testimonials can be written, rated or video depending upon the comfort of the client.

Important Tip:
Do offer a client a reward for a good testimonial to keep them motivated and engaged with it.

➢ By focusing on these strategies, salons can effectively differentiate themselves from competitors, build a loyal client base, and achieve long-term success in a competitive market. It is important to understand that competition is a good thing and it pushes us to constantly innovate and keep working out the best version of ourselves and our business.

❍ ❍ ❍ ❍

Chapter 6

Staff Motivation and Engagement: Crafting A Winning Team

Staff is the biggest key asset for your Salon Business. How well your salon runs or would do depends upon the quality, training, motivation and Human Resources policies that are applicable in the organisation. Motivating and engaging salon staff is crucial for ensuring high levels of performance, job satisfaction, and customer satisfaction.

Here are some effective strategies to keep your salon team members motivated and engaged:

1. ***Recognize and Reward Achievement***

   - ***Employee Recognition Programs:*** In order to make this effective it is important that there is a criteria for monitoring the performance of the team members. It is prudent to regularly acknowledge and reward staff for their hard work and achievements. This could include "**Employee of the Month**" awards, bonuses for reaching sales targets, or public recognition during team meetings. Some salons partner with brands to run staff motivation and training programs for their team members.
   - ***Incentives and Bonuses:*** Offer performance-based incentives, such as bonuses for meeting or exceeding service goals, retail sales, or customer retention targets. This encourages staff to consistently perform at their best. However, we should understand that while dealing with people there has to be some room for feedback and open and clear communication. The

performance of individuals cannot be the same and sometimes it's OK to get underperformance. The important thing is how we deal with such underperformance and how we provide feedback. It is important to understand their viewpoint also before drawing any conclusions. Just data alone should not be the parameter to arrive at the right decision.

2. ***Provide Opportunities for Growth and Development***

- ***Continuous Training:*** Invest in regular training and development programs to keep your staff updated on the latest industry trends, techniques, and products. This not only improves their skills but also shows that you're invested in their career growth. Such investments regularly motivate them and allow them to upgrade their skills. Please note that such opportunities build loyalty, and they will also differentiate you from all the other employers that they would have from time to time. They will always remember and cherish this gesture.
- ***Career Advancement Paths:*** Offer clear career progression paths, such as promoting stylists to senior roles or providing opportunities to become salon managers. This motivates employees to stay with the company long-term. There should be a clear organisation chart clear visibility and timely feedback on the performance and growth path. It may be frustrating to note that at times, without a clear visibility, it may lead to confusion and limit the mindset of the team when it comes to career path and progression.

3. ***Foster a Positive Work Environment***

- ***Open Communication:*** Encourage open communication between management and staff. It is important to hold executive meetings and open and clear communication and feedback channels to foster positivity and better organisation culture. It is important to note that there should be a mutual – both management and team decided – Slogan of the organisation that fosters progress and unites the purpose of the salon.

Also, regular investments in team building activities and celebrating employee special days is a good idea to build a positive work environment.

4. ***Offer Competitive Compensation and Benefits***

- ***Fair Compensation Structure:*** Ensure your staff is paid competitively as per the market norms, with salaries that reflect and are at market rates based on their experience and skill set. Consider offering incentives on services or retail products as an added incentive.
- ***Other Benefits and Perks:*** Providing benefits such as health insurance, life insurance, or employee discounts on services and products. These perks enhance job satisfaction and loyalty. When we implement these policies and procedures you will see a noticeable difference in their mindset and performance. It fosters a sense of security that they have some cover in case they face any emergency.

5. ***Be Transparent.***

Communication fosters trust, and both are two-way streets. The more information you can share regarding salon goals, progress and decisions, the more engaged and invested your staff will be. It is important to educate your team as to what it takes to run a business. Some of your employees might decide to open their own salon—and people who are motivated are going to leave anyway—but why not teach them about the expenses involved with keeping the business afloat? Plus, it helps all employees understand the big picture and the reasons behind some of your decisions. I think transparency is important because it helps the team understand what you go through while running a business and trying to remain profitable.

6. ***Have & Show a Caring Attitude.***

   Many employers find themselves mystified when an employee gives notice. That's because most staff members won't say anything unless asked. It's essential to do employee check-ins on a regular basis. In fact, let them know when you hire them that you're going to do this and that you want them to be candid. Ask, 'Is there anything you need from me?' and 'What can I do to make you more effective in your job?

   An attitude of caring tends to be contagious and encourages a more supportive atmosphere in the workplace overall. A person might share a challenge going on in her personal life with the team, and everyone can figure out together how to make things easier for that individual. Anything that lets your employees know you think about their work/life balance and not just what they can do for you shows you truly care.

   By implementing some of these strategies, you can create a motivated, engaged, and loyal team that is committed to delivering excellent service, and contributing to the growth and success of your salon business.

"SOMETIMES IT TAKES ONLY ONE ACT OF KINDNESS AND CARING TO CHANGE A PERSON'S LIFE".

\- JACKIE CHAN

Chapter 7

Choosing the Right Product and Brand

Most salons choose a product based on the salesperson who pitched them the product and offered a better discount.

In other cases, they choose based on local distributors' references.

Typically, these references are based on brands that offer them better margins and are often new/or relatively unknown brands.

It is important to consider whether the salesperson or distributor is trustworthy. What is the credibility they have in the market? Do not trust the source until you have surveyed the market and arrived at an informed decision.

Some important aspects in choosing the right brand can be as follows –

- Carefully pick the right brand in each category that has the capability to provide regular education, marketing, and logistics support.
- Picking the right brand partner is an extremely important step to realise the growth potential of your salon. Always mention your brand partners in your communications to build trust amongst your clients.
- A good brand partner will provide your team with regular education for the skill enhancement of your team.
- A good brand will keep in touch with you regularly and provide support as and when required.

- It is prudent to enter into a tiered agreement with the brand for the whole year, in order to have added benefits of education, merchandising, better discounts, deals and tiered benefits.
- Always check the logistics infrastructure of the brand and its track record for consistency of supplies and experience in the industry. You don't want to market products that are frequently out of stock!
- Launching innovative and new offerings from brands regularly will keep your clients engaged.
- Always plan the marketing calendar with the brand in advance. Using their network and activities can be another hook point in keeping your clients engaged and hooked to your salon regularly.
- Always check the education programs and the benefits the brand provides in skilling your team members. It is a proven fact that education is the most important tool for the salon business. While product education is important in knowing the science and SOP of different product lines, it is important that your team is also in the learning mode and is learning new skills, so they can upgrade themselves and help your salon to be more trending in your area, and hence make more money with the better and innovative offering.

Fun Fact

52.5% of the respondents have a relationship span with the salon for 1-3 Years

– Customer Loyalty is the Key!

Lure them with Exciting Services and Offers to keep them hooked!

This Isn't The End of The Road: Start An Exciting New Journey Forward

We are sure you have enjoyed reading this book, as much as we have enjoyed writing it. Most of the research in writing this book has been through meetings with salon owners on what it takes to run a successful salon.

We at Esskay Beauty, take pride that with our association thousands of salons have benefitted from our products and services and have grown their businesses.

Our focus has always been on honesty, transparency and having a long-term and ethical approach to dealing with all our stakeholders – Clients, Staff and Team Members.

We have been investing in strong research and development of newer and innovative products and have also been watching the global trends very closely to bring new innovations that can help and benefit salons in their entrepreneurial journey. Our core focus has always been on the highest product quality in all the brands and products that we choose to offer to our salon and distribution network.

Having a core focus on education and skill development programs that are run by highly trained, skilled and experienced faculty has helped us impart education to thousands of salon staff and helped them build a better life and earn more money. Our education programs are being imparted in our academies, online, events & seminars in hotels, tradeshows and inside the salons. We have also collaborated with international artists from Italy, Poland, the USA, etc., from time to time to bring in global education and exposure for our clients. Many more such collaborations are in the pipeline and continue to upgrade the Education standards in this industry.

Our *Tiered Tie Up* programs offer great rewards for all purchases made by the salon from our network offers rewards in the form of free products, education, year-end deals and benefits that help the salon owner get the best returns from the money they invest in products and also enables them in choosing the right brand partner.

Marketing has always been our core strength and we help advise on the marketing plans of the salons and assist them in planning and growing their business and acquiring and retaining clients.

We are available to talk to you and answer any queries that you may have whether you are running a salon or planning to open a new one.

Please feel free to write to us and fix up an appointment or a 30-minute Zoom call –

Ankit Virmani – ankit@esskaybeauty.com

Linked In: https://www.linkedin.com/in/ankitvirmani-in

Subham Virmani – sv@esskaybeauty.com

Linked In: https://www.linkedin.com/in/subham-virmani-57624b27/

For any queries or to tie up with our brands, please call +91 8882 800 800 or write to us on ***enquiry@esskaybeauty.com***

Here's a brief peek into Esskay Beauty

Esskay Beauty Resources Pvt Ltd, founded in 2002, started with humble beginnings from a small office in Central Delhi, today stands as a global leader in the beauty and wellness industry. With a bold vision of "Transforming Beauty and Wellness to the Next Level Globally," Esskay embodies the core values of Ethics, Passion, Responsibility, and Care, making it a standout family-managed business.

Headquartered in Gurgaon (Delhi NCR), Esskay has established a wide-reaching presence with distribution in 300 cities across 27 states in India and an expanding footprint in 3 countries. Their focus on education is evident through academies in Gurgaon and Education events across the country, nurturing the next generation of beauty professionals.

As the trusted channel partner for top international brands, Esskay has brought iconic names like Rica (Italy), Casmara (Spain), Olivia Garden (USA), and Macadamia (USA) to the Indian subcontinent.

Their business strategies have made Rica India's favourite wax, while Rica's Responsible Beauty line has set new standards in sustainable hair colour and care. Esskay's portfolio also includes its own exclusive brands like Skinora for professional skincare, Mr Barber for innovative hair tools, and Ola! Candy for vibrant nail colours and accessories.

With over 12 products sold every minute, Esskay Beauty Resources is recognized globally as a leader in professional salon distribution. The company's excellence was celebrated with the prestigious Femina Power Brand Award in 2021. Known for fostering strong partnerships with key players in the salon industry, Esskay continues to set benchmarks in innovation, quality, and sustainability.

This powerhouse company is not only shaping the beauty industry in India but is also creating lasting impacts on a global scale.